Talking Hands

AT SCHOOL

EN LA ESCUELA

The Child's World

Published in the United States of America by The Child's World®
PO Box 326, Chanhassen, MN 55317-0326
800-599-READ
www.childsworld.com

Cover: left, right, back—Brand X Pictures; frontispiece: left, right—Brand X Pictures.

Interior: 2, 7, 8, 18, 19, 20, 21, 23—Brand X Pictures; 3, 6, 9, 10, 11, 12, 14, 15, 16, 17—Stockdisc/Getty Images; 4—S. Meltzer/PhotoLink/Photodisc/Getty Images; 5—PhotoLink/Photodisc/Getty Images; 13—Corbis; 22—Michael Matisse/Photodisc/Getty Images.

The Child's World®: Mary Berendes, Publishing Director

Editorial Directions, Inc.: E. Russell Primm, Editorial Director; Katie Marsico, Managing Editor; Judith Shiffer, Associate Editor; Caroline Wood, Editorial Assistant; Javier Millán, Proofreader; Cian Laughlin O'Day, Photo Researcher and Selector

The Design Lab: Kathleen Petelinsek, Art Director; Julia Goozen, Art Production

LIBRARY OF CONGRESS CATALOGING-IN-PUBLICATION DATA
Petelinsek, Kathleen.
  At school = En la escuela / by Kathleen Petelinsek and
E. Russell Primm.
    p. cm. — (Talking hands)
  In English and Spanish.
  ISBN 1-59296-450-8 (lib. bdg. : alk. paper)
  1. American Sign Language—Juvenile literature. 2. Public school—
Juvenile literature. I. Title: En la escuela. II. Primm, E. Russell, 1958– III. Title.
  HV2476.P472 2006
  419'.7—dc22   2005027104

NOTE TO PARENTS AND EDUCATORS:

The understanding of any language begins with the acquisition of vocabulary, whether the language is spoken or manual. The books in the Talking Hands series provide readers, both young and old, with a first introduction to basic American Sign Language signs. Combining close photo cues and simple, but detailed, line illustration, children and adults alike can begin the process of learning American Sign Language. In addition to the English word and sign for that word, we have included the Spanish word. The addition of the Spanish word is a wonderful way to allow children to see multiple ways (English, Spanish, signed) to say the same word. This is also beneficial for Spanish-speaking families to learn the sign even though they may not know the English word for that object.

Let these books be an introduction to the world of American Sign Language. Most languages have regional dialects and multiple ways of expressing the same thought. This is also true for sign language. We have attempted to use the most common version of the signs for the words in this series. As with any language, the best way to learn is to be taught in person by a frequent user. It is our hope that this series will pique your interest in sign language.

Bus
Autobús

1.

2.

3.

3

School
Escuela

1.

With left palm up and right palm down, clap hands together twice.

Con la palma izquierda hacia arriba y la palma derecha hacia abajo, aplauda las manos dos veces.

4

Class
Clase

1.

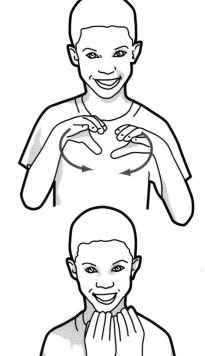

2.

Hands make the letter "C" while making a circle.

Las manos hacen la letra "C" mientras que hacen un círculo.

5

Backpack
Mochila

1.

Tap chest with thumbs.

Golpee ligeramente el pecho con los pulgares.

6

Desk
Escritorio

1.

Right arm moves down and taps left arm twice.

El brazo derecho baja y golpea ligeramente el brazo izquierdo dos veces.

Chair
Silla

1.

2.

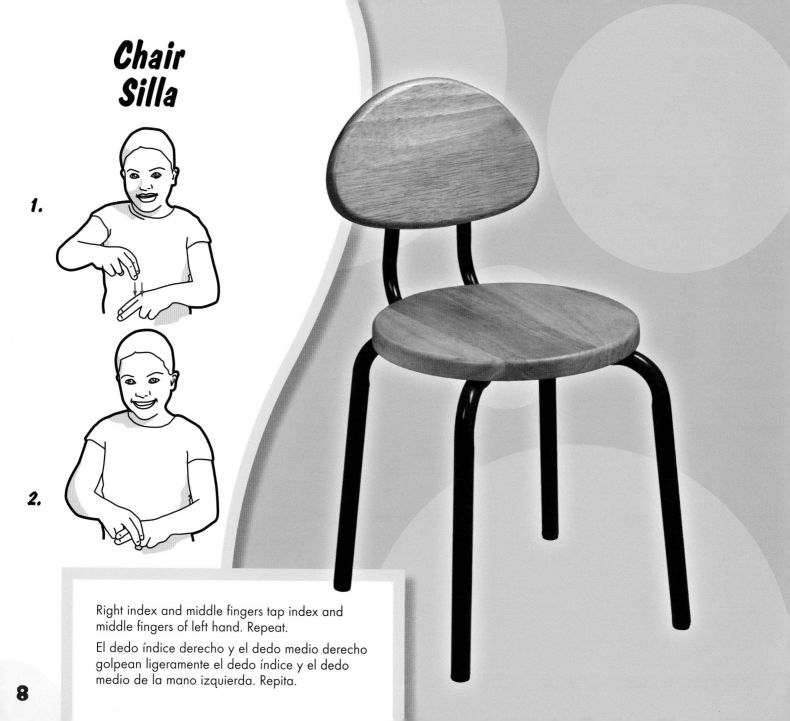

Right index and middle fingers tap index and middle fingers of left hand. Repeat.

El dedo índice derecho y el dedo medio derecho golpean ligeramente el dedo índice y el dedo medio de la mano izquierda. Repita.

Student
Estudiante

1.

2.

3.

For steps one and two, close fingers of right hand as it moves from palm of left hand to forehead.

Para el primer y segundo paso, cierra los dedos de la mano derecha a la misma vez que se mueve de la palma de la mano izquierda hacia la frente.

Teacher
Maestra

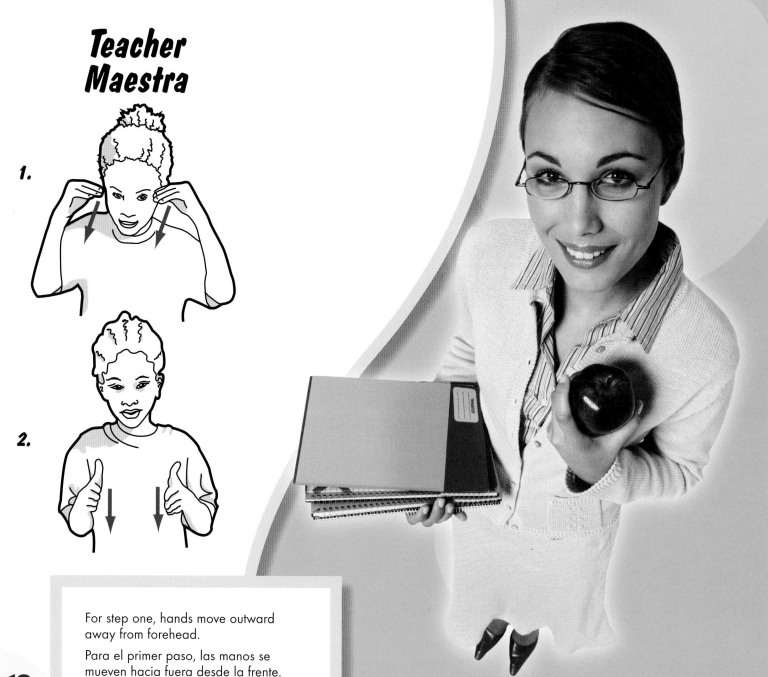

1.

2.

For step one, hands move outward away from forehead.

Para el primer paso, las manos se mueven hacia fuera desde la frente.

Computer
Computadora

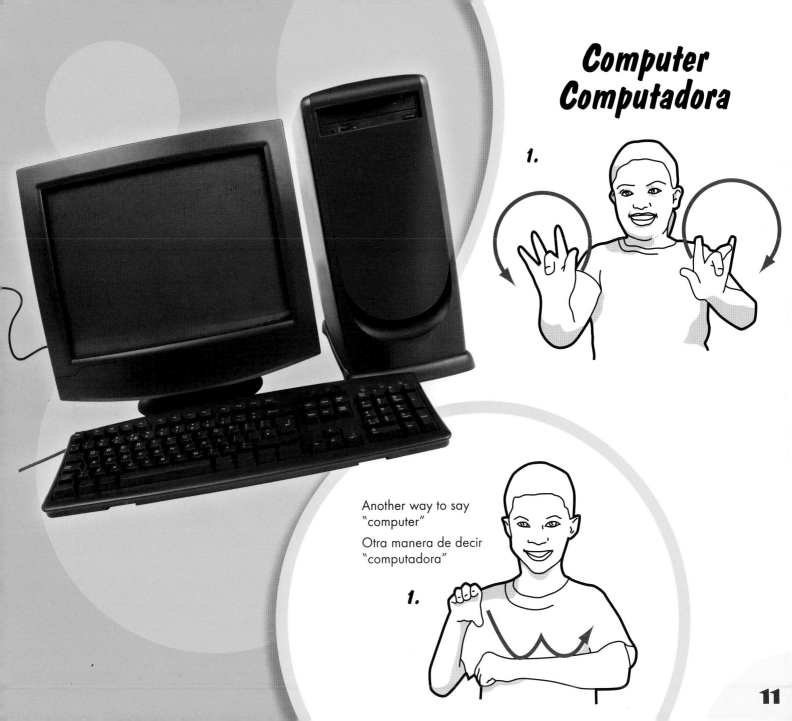

1.

Another way to say "computer"

Otra manera de decir "computadora"

1.

Book
Libro

1.

2.

Open hands as if opening a book. Repeat.
Abra las manos como si abriera un libro. Repita.

Library
Biblioteca

1.

Hillsmere Elementary
Media Center

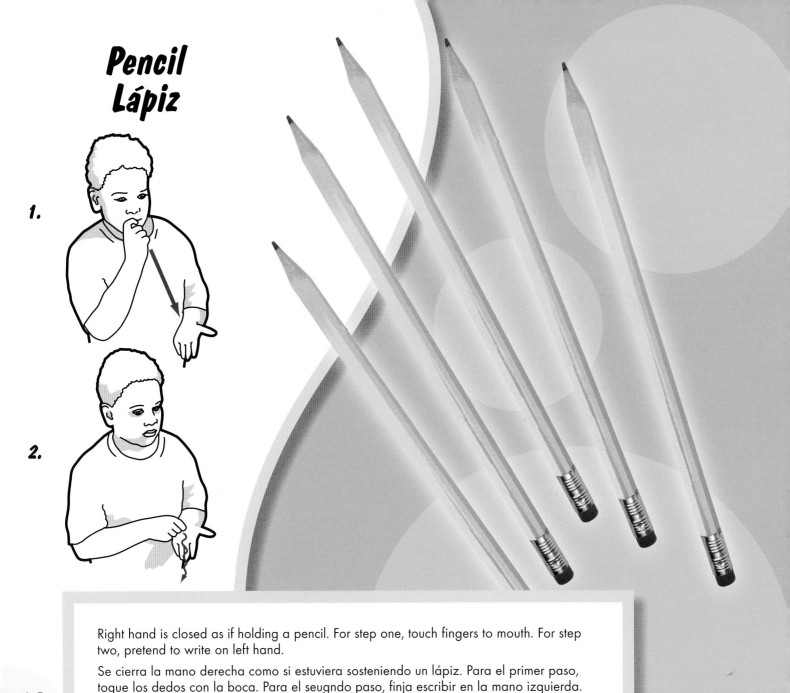

Pencil
Lápiz

1.

2.

Right hand is closed as if holding a pencil. For step one, touch fingers to mouth. For step two, pretend to write on left hand.

Se cierra la mano derecha como si estuviera sosteniendo un lápiz. Para el primer paso, toque los dedos con la boca. Para el seugndo paso, finja escribir en la mano izquierda.

14

Paper
Papel

1.

Right hand diagonally taps left hand twice.

La mano derecha diagonalmente golpea ligeramente la mano izquierda dos veces.

Paint
Pintura

1.

2.

Right hand moves up and down, similar to a paintbrush, against left hand.

La mano derecha se mueve hacia arriba y hacia abajo, similar como una brocha, contra la mano izquierda.

Glue
Pegamento

1.

Right hand makes the letter "G" and moves from palm to fingers over left hand twice.

La mano derecha hace la letra "G" y se mueve dos veces desde la palma hasta los dedos sobre la mano izquierda.

17

Scissors
Tijera

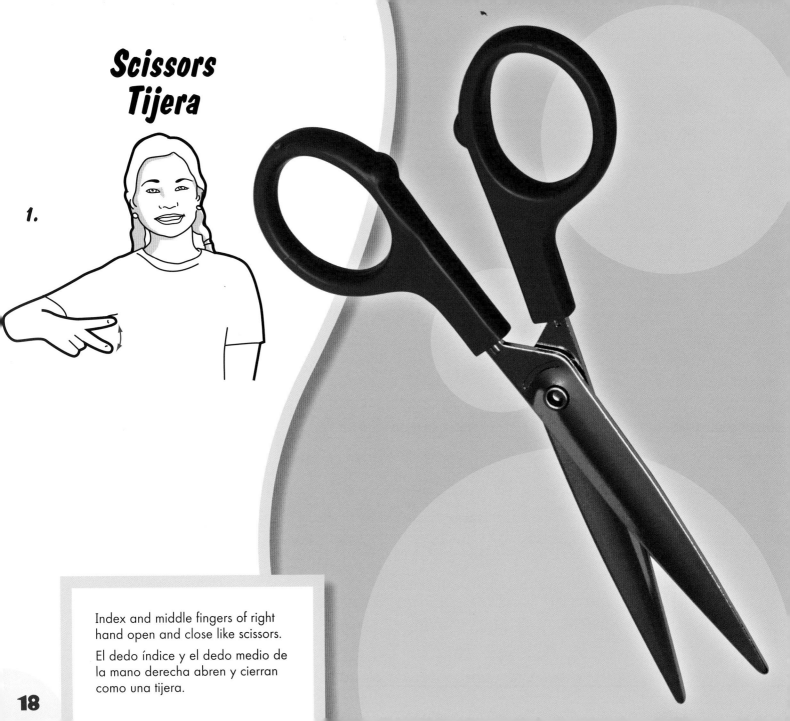

1.

Index and middle fingers of right hand open and close like scissors.

El dedo índice y el dedo medio de la mano derecha abren y cierran como una tijera.

Eraser
Borrador

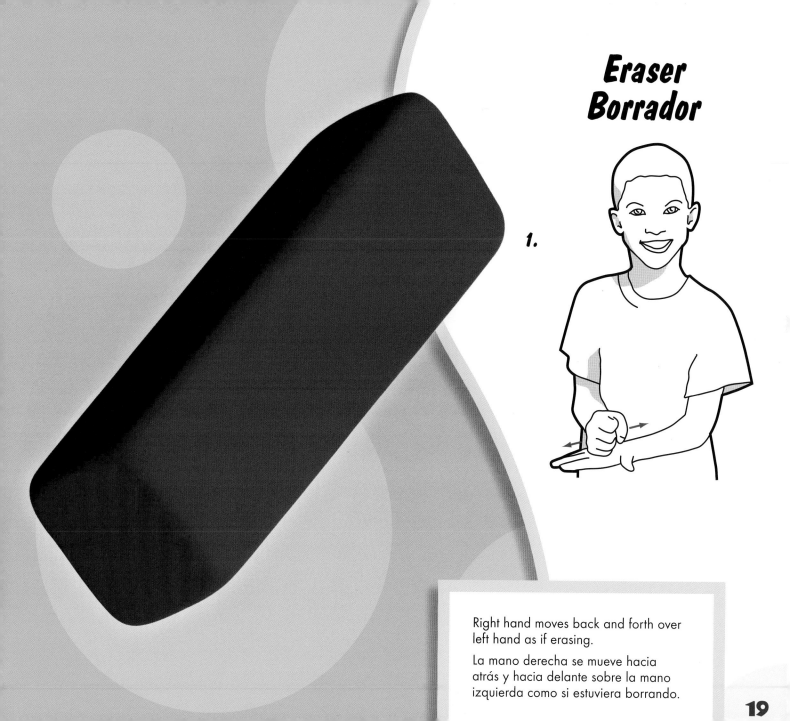

1.

Right hand moves back and forth over left hand as if erasing.

La mano derecha se mueve hacia atrás y hacia delante sobre la mano izquierda como si estuviera borrando.

Crayon
Creyón

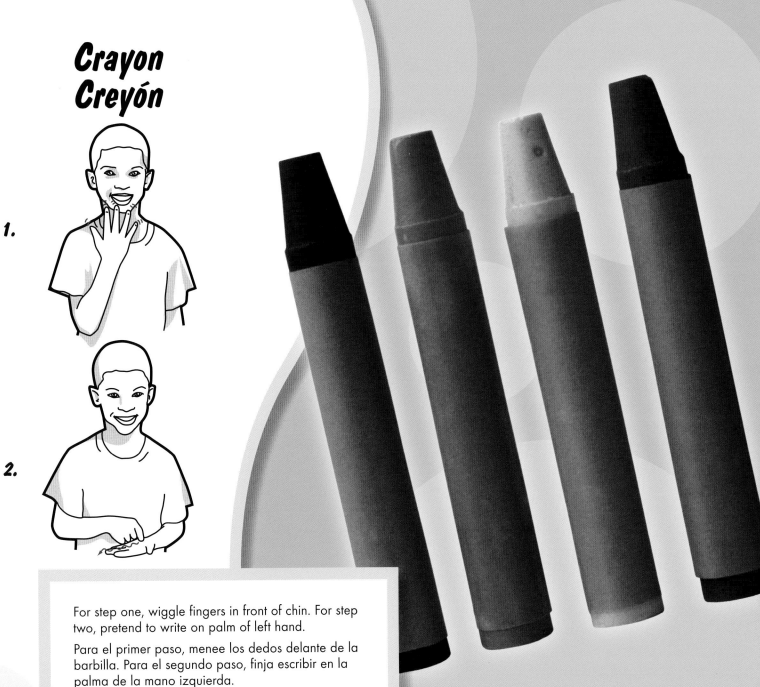

1.

2.

For step one, wiggle fingers in front of chin. For step two, pretend to write on palm of left hand.

Para el primer paso, menee los dedos delante de la barbilla. Para el segundo paso, finja escribir en la palma de la mano izquierda.

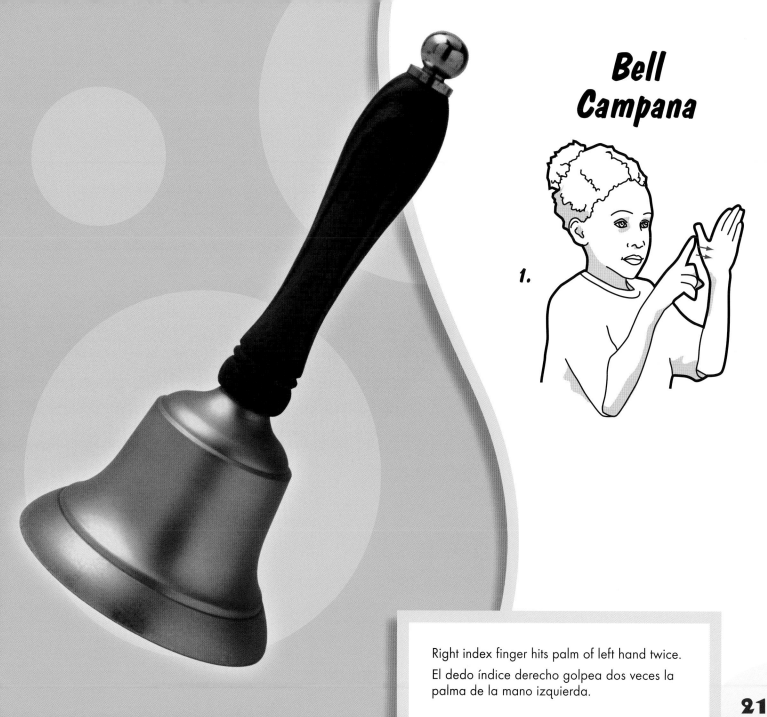

Bell
Campana

1.

Right index finger hits palm of left hand twice.

El dedo índice derecho golpea dos veces la palma de la mano izquierda.

Playground
Patio

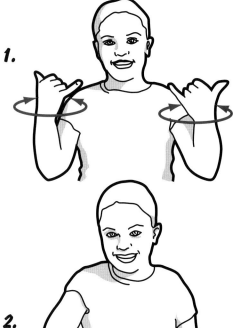

1.

2.

For step one, hands make the letter "Y" and twist back and forth. For step two, move open hand in counterclockwise circle.

Para el primer paso, las manos hacen la letra "Y" y tuercen hacia adelante y hacia atrás. Para el segundo paso, mueva la mano abierta en círculo de izquierda a derecha.

Clock
Reloj

1.

2.

For step one, right index finger taps left wrist.

Para el primer paso, el dedo índice derecho golpea ligeramente la muñeca izquierda.

A B C D E F

G H I J K

L M N O P

Q R S T U

V W X Y Z

A SPECIAL THANK-YOU

to our models from the Alexander Graham Bell Elementary School in Chicago, Illinois:

Alina is seven years old and is in the second grade. Her favorite things to do are art, soccer, and swimming. DJ is her brother!

Dareous has seven brothers and sisters. He likes football. His favorite team is the Detroit Lions. He also likes to play with his Gameboy and Playstation.

Darionna is seven and is in the second grade. She has two sisters. She likes the swings and merry-go-round on the play-ground. She also loves art.

DJ is eight years old and is in the third grade. He loves playing the harmonica and his Gameboy. Alina is his sister!

Jasmine is seven years old and is in the second grade. She likes writing and math in school. She also loves to swim.